Sunrise at Midnight

BY:

MIK

Charleston, SC

www.PalmettoPublishing.com

Sunrise at Midnight

Copyright © 2021 by MIK

First Edition

ISBN: 978-1-63837-844-0

ebook ISBN: 978-1-63837-845-7

This is my story. The raw, the real, the rugged. I thank those who have stayed by my side, encouraged me, and helped me see how beautiful this life can be.

I tell my story as a way to express who I am, who I have become, and who I have let go within to become the woman I am.

You are never alone, I am with you and within the stars

To the complicated, confusing, and impossible:
Sunrise at Midnight

Trigger Warning Advised

I hope by the time you're reading this
if you ever do
That I no longer love you

Purple and pink nightgown

When I was too young to understand
Hands touched me in places and I
think that's where most of my trauma
began
He touched me in places I had yet to
learn the proper names for
Innocence bought out like a discount
in the store
I hated those colors for years,
blaming them for being too girly
Too girly?
An excuse for what he did to me
It took me years to find my voice and
scream "I'm free"

Pink still makes me feel uneasy
And when it covers my skin I feel
queasy
Remnants of the man I did not choose
to please
I close it deep inside my closet to
give me ease
But now purple gives me power,
It takes away the hurt and lets me
feel as beautiful and as delicate as
a flower
Grown from dirt, in the broken seams
of concrete
I scratched and clawed to find a way
back to my own heartbeat

Rain speckles the windowpane quietly
as the storm rolls in
Gazing out all I see are hues of
grey dripping from the sky as I wait
for the thunder to begin
I feel the loneliness within each
rumble just like it bellows within
my heart
Now it's pouring as the clouds fall
apart
They could no longer carry the
weight of their own sadness, I can
feel its sobs with each trembling
wind it breathes
I wait for it to blow over, but the
storm inside never truly leaves

As I watch you smile at me I feel a
cold presence caress my face
I wonder how quickly you'll just
become another moment, a time, a
place
I wonder how long it will take until
you notice the first thing that you
hate
When I'll become just okay instead
of great
Something that will begin the weight
of unease,
Knowing that you'll become too hard
to please
You'll learn my buttons and I'll sew
myself shut
Your words will become sharp and
you'll know exactly where to cut
I don't want to let you in
I know how this goes and I never win
You feel so warm but I feel myself
getting cold
Running away from the security of
the structure before it begins to
unfold

Without bad days
We would never know what good days
are

How can you ever feel loved when
you've never truly known love?
How do you know what love is when no
love has been kind to you?

It's the fact that I've had more gas
station cashiers ask me how my day
is going more than my parents have
my entire life
It's the fact that my neighbor stops
by every now and then because she
was worried that I haven't been out
for a while
I don't know if my parents have ever
stopped by just because
It's the fact that my friends invite
me over for dinner more times than
I've had a family dinner
It's the fact that my boss bandaged
my wounds and asked me if I was
alright when all my life I was told
to suck it up
It's the fact that more strangers
passing me on the street stop to see
if I'm okay instead of ignoring me
for days
How can you deny the feeling of
being unwanted?

Stop being a doormat for someone who
won't even hold the door for you

Will you ever let me free?

I feel your memories holding me
hostage
The way you would touch me so softly
I feel it wrapped around my throat
Your presence sticks to me like a
winter coat
But you don't keep me warm anymore
I don't have your love in store
I catch myself wondering if you're
thinking of me
If you're telling her all of the
things we were supposed to be
If you look her in the eyes and tell
her the same sweet lies
Every time I pass a fast car
I wonder where you are
Even with the wind in my hair, my
fists to the air
When I'm dancing around with
strangers to fill your void
The sound of your voice playing in
my head crashes in like an asteroid

You tell me you wish I was there
You say you miss the curls in my
hair
You ask me how it's possible to be
with someone but thinking of me

Will you ever let me free?

I replied baby I don't know, but
it's torture
I almost felt you get a little
warmer
But the flame blew out, left me on
read
There are so many things I wish you
would have said
I keep my distance, a pretty bird on
its perch
Wishing you'd swoop down and take me
to that church
The one you said you could hear our
bells ringing
They'll say here comes the bride,
but I'll be on the side singing

I watch her live the life you
promised to me
An unsettled ground catastrophic to
be

Will you ever let me free?

I try so desperately to hate you, I
wish more than ever to be free
But I feel you, I feel you still
holding out to me
I try to sever you off, but I'm the
only one to bleed
You will never give me what I need
A lonely woman in the shallows of
the night
Still out searching for her lost
knight
Her freedom caged inside a man who
does not care
She's teetering back from the ledge,
a bird ready to take air

I used to cry myself to sleep
Just wanting you to come to bed with
me
So I could feel your warmth
Feel loved
But you'd stay in the front room
occupied
And come to bed long after my eyes
finally closed
But you never noticed the wetness on
my cheeks

Life is a constantly changing
variable that everyone is trying to
solve for

There are broken people with good
intentions
There are broken people with bad
intentions

I wish I could stay here in paradise
Try our love and bet on luck like
we're throwing dice
Snake eyes; one is me one is you
We were splashing and laughing, the
ocean was so blue
The shower, the bed
I try but I can't get you out of my
head
I feel myself slipping and letting
these feelings take me
I know that is hopeless to wish
that we were meant to be
You plant me with such excitement
and arousal
Your touch makes me dizzy and I
don't want to get off your carousel
I know we'll say goodbye and go our
separate ways
But please don't forget me and our
mid-October days
And when I look up at the lonely
night sky
I'll smile at the stars
and recall the times of you and I
Sparkling through the chaos and
confusion
Wanting to be with you will forever
be my biggest delusion

I loved the way he touched me
Every touch felt explosive, taking
me higher
And higher

I feel as though I am a prisoner in
my own rib cage
Held hostage by all things that
haunt me
Suffocating in a bed of hands
grabbing at my throat
Their claws tearing through my veins
Bound and whipped by their chains
The scared tremor of my heart
Screaming as every little thing rips
me apart
My own heart causing an earthquake
I give and I give and they take and
they take
You pick and feed off of me like you
did Prometheus
You make me out to be Medusa when
you turned my sickness into a
sinking stone
I am fucking drowning I feel no God
has got me now
I will slip through the cracks of
Heaven like dirty water in a storm
drain
You did this to me, you caused this
pain

I wonder if you ever think of me
Or if I'm easy to forget while
you're lying in her bed

You see, I loved him.
I loved him wildly, freely,
intensely, yet gently
I loved him deeper than the depths
of the ocean that I cried my tears
into
I loved him more ferociously than
the soul of a volcano that bubbled
and oozed with rage
I loved his complexion more than I
loved my own reflection
I would admire him for hours and
wonder how on Earth he could be mine

But the reality is, he wasn't
He did not love me
He would repeat it back like an echo
down a hall
As if to appease me but deep down I
knew it all
The lies that coated his lips when
he would kiss me softly
Even when I knew the truth
I let him treat me like shit and
acted bulletproof

Honey, why do you feed me lies?
Why can't you tell me the truth when
you look deep into my eyes?
After everything I've done and did
Yet you still choose to run around
and play me like a kid

I laid there
Breathing the scent of fresh Earth
Grass has yet to cover you in a
plush blanket
I sing you songs softly,
Ones we would sing in the car
Ones you looked me in the eyes and
kissed me to
My tears softly pool in the dirt
I close my eyes curled on your grave
Remembering how it felt with you
wrapped behind me
My hair is now matted with mud from
my tears wetting the loose dirt
Flowers lie with me, wilting in the
cold
Fake flowers above your head like a
broken crown
How do you choose a headstone for a
king
Stolen in the night
I wish I could have loved you in all
the ways I had wanted
And all the ways you more than
deserved
I feel so hollow

Sometimes these things, these
memories, these nightmares, they
come back for me
They nip at my heels like hungry
wolves wanting to rip the tendons
out from under my cold skin and hang
me from a weeping willow
My own flesh and blood causing me to
kick my feet in a cynical dance
The wolves mimic with wicked grins
as they kick snow with their strong
back legs like a cat covering its
tracks
They're covering the red melting
snow with more pure white, howling
with laughter while I dance for air

Last night I dreamed of you, it is
still so fresh in my mind,
dangling in front of me like a ripe
fruit ready to be plucked
You kissed me softly, it was as
delicious as the first bite of a
crisp apple
I savored each sweet bite, letting
it drip down my chin
It is such a guilty pleasure to wake
up and have not even had your hands
on me, only the you I see in my
dreams and have my sheets spell out
exactly what you do to me
Your hands around me, my body around
you, my mind spinning around in a
dizzy daze, my body overcome with a
dancing haze, only knowing that I
never want it to stop
For just you, only you.

You make me feel like the golden
sunlight that spills and drips
across an old wooden floor, giving
it luster despite the beating it's
taken over years of being walked all
over

Because it burns in my throat like
bile and cries me to sleep
Labels
We often grow used to having labels
thrown at us
It's like a broken machine that
keeps spitting out papers
We pick up each paper and read it
Each word stays with us
But we pretend it doesn't
And we move on to pick up the next
label
She's a label
Stamped with words like a pad of
paper you practice dropping ink onto

I want to blame them for not being
there for me
No mother or father I felt as
though I could lean on
Booze and absence was what I
thought love consisted of

It's not that I didn't love you
Oh no
I loved you far too much
I never wanted to leave you
I had to leave because you never
deserved me

What is it truly?
What is it that knocks me to my
knees rocking and reeling on a
rollercoaster engrossed with my own
self-loathing?
Is it truly that I am not enough,
or is it that I do not give myself
enough?
I tell myself that I am short change
for a dollar, that I do not make any
sense
Yet I fail to pay up to my own
worth, I decline my card before it
ever swipes through the reader
Am I myself the reader or do I let
the world swallow my currency as
if a vicious current that sucks me
under, yet I dare to cry out that I
cannot breathe under the waters I
have allowed myself to be trapped
beneath
I pace and try to declare that, I
too have a place!
Yet, I have no trophy to award
myself when I am the only one in the
race
Is it that I have no credit or is it
that I have put myself in debt?

A debt of doubt and hatred for the very beat beneath my chest and I never slow down to give my mind a moment of rest
I chase my own tail and then wonder why I cannot catch it
I must not be quick enough, I must not be trying my best
But what would really happen if I caught it? Then what's next?
Would I sit there jaws clenched biting down onto myself feeling relieved?
That for once I could proclaim, I can succeed?
What would happen if I let myself be?
If I did not tear her apart into shreds and then try to frantically place the pieces back together while the jagged edges slice me like paper into two
I can't help but wonder if I'm living for me or for you
"You" as in the false proclaimed identity of the world and what it views me to be
What do I view myself as? Why can't I be nice to her for all she has done for me?

I want to smash my head until
all remnants of my thoughts are
splattered

I'd be lying if I said I no longer
loved you
I just try my best to remember why I
should hate you

Sometimes my hands ache to comfort
them
A slight touch on the back to feel
not so alone
Sometimes I can see it in their eyes
Sometimes they're hollow
Sometimes they're dark
Sometimes I can see tears that will
never fall
Sometimes I wonder how long it's
been since they've been caressed
Since they've been held when their
head or tummy hurts
I wonder where the line gets drawn
in a young boys life
Where he's not supposed to be held
anymore
Or kissed on the forehead
Or told he's loved and appreciated

Her body was succulent, ripe, and
juicy like a peach
I saw her looking at me in my
favorite tree and I knew I had to
make her mine
The taste of her sweet surrender to
me dripped down my chin
Sweet peaches against my lips, a
taste dancing with my tongue
Moving together in an orchestra
of sound composed from my energy
becoming a catalyst for hers
Deep, deep harmonies combined into
one undeniable tone of pleasure
My hunger to taste the sticky
sweetness of her tickles my mind

I choose to love you from a
distance, still admiring the fire
Knowing it will scar me if I touch
it again
So I watch another woman become your
gasoline and try to stay clear of
the explosion
I was once the victim of your
terrorism, you scattered me
And I'm still picking up the pieces

You're as sweet as the brownie
batter we made
Your laughter was richer than the
chocolate itself as I let you lick
the spoon

You see
Everyone leaves
Every goodbye, every I'll see you
later, every I'm just going to the
gas station
Turns into a ticking time clock of
their actual departure
Every farewell closer to the finale
You see no one has ever stayed
Each time someone leaves they come
back different
More distant
More unsure
More dissociated
How can you ever be convinced that
someone loves you and will be with
you no matter what when the very
people that created you never come
around?
That inside your head is this awful,
dreary sound

The unease, the panic
Convinced someone would be happier
without me around because everyone
who left must have not loved me and
if you do not love someone why would
you stay?
So they go
And I watch them leave just like I
did for the first formative years of
my life
I hear the engine rumble and laugh
at me for thinking someone would
stay
I hold my breath until I can no
longer see their car
And then I collapse
Crying on the floor because I'm alone
again
My tears write the list of things
people leave me for, for things they
love more
Alcohol, money, and someone behind a
closed door

I feel like I won't ever heal
from this
I don't want to keep dragging you
down
I don't want to keep bringing it up
It bubbles inside of me
It feels like hell is burning
within me
I try to swallow it, but it burns
so badly
Why can't we just talk about it?

Who the fuck hurt you so badly?
Who the fuck ripped you open and
shredded you to pieces like a once
perfectly wrapped gift that's now
a crumpled mess on the floor being
kicked around?

Get UP

Sprawled on my back, the stars in
the sky started connecting the dots
There are constellations in my eyes
It was snowing
Flakes of white sprinkled across my
face like freckles
I'm numb.
I'm so numb it makes my pupils
dilate opening a portal into another
universe
Snow angels in my numbness waving
hello
My smile spreading across my face as
my body takes off into the atmosphere
My energy is skyrocketing
I'm chasing shooting stars

I don't know how to make friends
I feel so out of place
I never learned to play nice
All I knew was to not trust others
To protect yourself and turn away
from the world

We walk along this trail
Not knowing what to do
Not knowing what to say
My throat has been torn out,
No way to speak what's on my mind
We've walked along many trails,
But this one is new
One where we are no longer connected
A whole torn in half
My heart aches for how badly you
want me
My heart aches for how wrong you did
me
Our hands brush, the memories
The memories of our hands
interlocked skips across my mind,
but I ignore
We are now only friends, once
passionate lovers
Not knowing what to do
Not knowing what to say

I dream of you at night
A dizzy daze that fogs my sense of
reality and I see you
I become paralyzed, the mist tickles
my dark eyelashes and drips like
tears from my star-speckled eyes
It drips the same way morning dew
rolls off the fresh earth
It drips like the soft glow of your
sweat as you looked down at me
smiling
I feel you in my dreams, holding me
once more
I sink into your safety wrapped in
the covers

This monster within me
It paces
It shreds apart pretty faces
I feel it groan and howl in pain
Screaming as the darkness reaps
within its soul
Screaming within my soul as its
darkness reaps
A seizure foaming
Jerking erratically contorting and
heaving
Letmefuckinggo
It's hungry now
Unable to feed itself
A wicked tooth grin, I am a tasty
treat
Hunger deeper than my hollowed eyes
Jesus Christ, can't you hear my
screams laying within my cries?
I am bleeding through my eyes
Watch them disappear, rock back into
my head
All I see is red
Bash my fists against the pavement
Mimicking the soft drop of a
splattered teardrop
My pulse splattered, anything to
beat it back into place
I can't erase his face

My soul coats me as if a coal mine
I leave my mess everywhere I go
Please don't slip into my mind
It will eat you alive
Hungry handed child
Her cries suffocate me
Let me be, let me be
I am starved
It boils and bubbles within me like
lava
I am a volcano
This is the meltdown
It burns
please help I am burning alive
It jumps up to my throat
A wildfire within me
Watch an innocent doe being eaten
within its claws
Tell me how that is fair
The words I speak, hardly compare
The beast that crawls and clings
Is a creation of all beings
How do you kill it I haven't a clue
because
How do you silence all that became
of you?

Why do you make excuses for someone
else's own incompetence?

I will never read through someone's
messages again
If I think I need too
I'll just walk away and let him
lose what he thought he'd win

you never loved me.
It's as simple and disastrous as that
You *never* loved me
I was convenient
As easy as the first gas station at
the closest exit
A quick stop to piss me away and
never look back
An infatuated feeling of forced
emotions
You never loved me
So now I rid myself of you
It is never as simple as cutting ties
Years too long of confusion and
begging,
I must slowly unravel this braided
mess that has wound itself around my
throat and held me captive within my
mind

It's knotted, matted, twisted, and
tangled
It's hurting me
But I will undo your damage
I will find myself once again
The thing you underestimated the
most was in fact, me
You must have thought you could keep
a hold on the "broken girl"
Fuck you for saying that, by the way
But I have been damaged far worse
than you
And survived
I am thriving without you feeding me
your poison
And I will never cry for another fix

Your eyes changed suddenly
As if they were embers in a fire and
the wind had just stirred them
Giving them enough oxygen to catch
fire once more
I remember feeling like the same
thing had happened to me
not in my eyes
but my soul.

Brown eyed beauty,
Showing me love without cruelty
A peacock in full bloom
A pattern weaving within my loom
Midnight cinnamon rolls and wine
You're my forbidden fruit plucked off
the ripest vine
A voice of the wind
Sending me on a whim
A beauty with brown eyes
Gentle enough to hush my cries
Your success is enough to despise
You hold me high above your head
Never caring of how I have been
taken or led
An understanding soul comprised of
my favorite nights
A summer high taken to new heights

I didn't get to count your ten
fingers and ten toes
I didn't get to kiss you on your
little nose
I didn't get to hold you tight
I didn't get to tell you goodnight
Your departure has left me broken-
hearted
You left me just as things started
I never got to give your name
thought
I never got to see who's eyes you
got
Would you have been short or tall?
How long would it have taken you
before you could crawl?
You were a blessing that was issued
and then recalled
A plane that had just taken off and
then stalled
He didn't want you as I did,
"I can't take care of you let alone
a kid"

But it's okay, mommy loved you so
More than I could tell you or you
would ever know
I don't know where you are now, with
God or in the stars
But please know in my heart you were
ours
I could've done it on my own
I would've never let you felt alone
But you left me without warning
And now I'm left mourning
I didn't get to hear your innocent
laugh
I didn't get to see myself reflected
as your half
I didn't get to feel your finger wrap
around mine
I don't know if I'll ever be fine
I have a hole left in my chest
And trust me I'm trying my best
But I feel like when I lost you, you
took me with you

I sat there
Playing a soft melody
Hoping that the gentle sound would
drift your way and make you
remember me
My fingertips lightly danced on each
key
Remnants of my last plea
To touch and hold you one last time
For you to forever be mine
Hoping my tune would let me fill
your void
You left me with a crater in my
heart, it hit me like an asteroid
My music fades within the breeze,
almost as quickly as you forgot
about me

Unraveling, spiraling, and spilling
into spindles of twine
My head is reeling but I smile and
say I am fine
I see the hunger in his eyes and I'm
starving for a feel
I don't care if it isn't real

I think I'll miss you forever
Time with you is greater than any
treasure
My tears wouldn't stop falling as
the plane took flight
I look down watching you disappear
and none of it feels right
I don't want to go back to the
place I don't belong
A place where no one loves me and
everything is wrong
A place obsessed with the past, no
understanding
I can feel my happiness crash
landing
I am engulfed in flames and
completely destroyed
I don't think anything could fill
this void

I think of you and close my eyes
oh my
I take my hands and trace all the
places you like to touch
oh my
I think of your mouth on me, your
tongue within me
oh my
I take my delicate fingertips and
touch myself to the rhythm of the
last time you gave yourself to me
oh my
I think of us finishing together as
we have so many times before I go
oh my oh my oh my

You buzz around in my mind
Thoughts of you in my flower bed fly,
My sweet nectar drips down my thigh
Sweet, sweet, honey
You're my hardest goodbye

Angel eyes, baby blues swimming in
the sea
I was a lost ship, casted out
Waiting for you to capsize me

Dear future lover,
I'm sorry
There are so many parts of me that
you may never understand
Please don't fall in love with me if
you don't understand
Dear future lover,
I'm sorry sometimes I flinch when you
reach out to love me, a man that
"loved" me left marks to prove that
it wasn't true, black and blue that
screamed out "I hate you"
Dear future lover, I'm sorry that
sometimes I rock and reel, spinning
out of control and trying to grasp
the way I feel
Dear future lover, I'm sorry that
sometimes I worry about your
friends, a man that "loved" me left
me for my best friend and said that
I was just practice in the end
Dear future lover, I'm sorry
sometimes it feels like there's an
elephant on my chest, it's hard to
breathe even when I try my best

Dear future lover, I'm sorry that
sometimes I seem cold to your touch,
a man that "loved" me wouldn't
listen to me as I begged no, and now
I have more scars in places that I
don't show

Dear future lover, I'm sorry I don't
trust you, my love life has always
been made of lies, texts full of
alibis, and at the end of the night
my tears singing their own lonely
lullabies

Dear future lover, I'm sorry I worry
too much. A man I loved never came
home, fell asleep at the wheel and
my tears streamed through a black
veil

Dear future lover, I'm sorry I'm so
quiet. The last man I let in my life
silenced my soul, he took my love
and burned it like coal

Dear future lover, I'm sorry I
feel so ugly. No amount of lingerie
could keep him from becoming a stray
looking for a free bone and leaving
me worried at home

Dear future lover, I'm sorry I ask
you if your food is okay, he used to
let dinner go cold while he would
play and then tell me that it wasn't
quite made the right way
Dear future lover, I'm sorry I don't
like my body. I read texts to dozens
of women that were not me, hearing
every word of everything I always
wanted to be
Dear future lover, I'm sorry I let
these things happen to me, you never
realize how messy it can be until
you say it out loud, sometimes I
feel like I'm screaming in a room
full of people and no one looks up
from the crowd
Dear future lover, I'm sorry I say
sorry too much I use it as my crutch
when I'm broken inside
I apologize if I run from your love
and hide
Dear future lover, I'm not easy,
my stomach turns to knots and I
get queasy at the slightest change
in your voice or movement I know
that I need to work on my own self-
improvement

Dear future lover, sometimes I get so sad, I try so hard to let go of the things I had but oftentimes they creep back into my head and I'll stay wrapped up in covers frozen in bed

Dear future lover, if you love me, love me. From A to Z head to toe, I promise I won't let you go, I have so much love to give and have a tendency to over forgive

Dear future lover don't take advantage of my heart, I'll let you in if you promise to not tear me apart

Just promise to not leave
I need your arms around me in order to believe
That real love exists in more than just stories
And that you can help me fix all of my worries

I did a trust fall and opened my
eyes to a knife stuck through my
chest
How torturing it is to have a heart
that loves you, and a brain that
knows better

I admired and adored you like the
rare, delicate Juliet Rose
But in fact, you were poison ivy and
my skin still crawls when I think of
what you did

I feel so suffocated
Like I need to burst out of an
invisible box

A relentless repeat of normality

You remind me of rain in the desert,
unexpected, unpredicted, but so
unimaginably good
You tickle my nose with sprinkles
of love and kindness, you water
my parched, cracking tongue, a
waterfall of words now running
through the seals of my mouth
You move dancing like the
electricity that pulses through my
skies, emitting flashes of lights
that dazzle me
You struck me with your heart, your
pain, you bleed out and onto me,
into me, two seas meeting, still
separated but moving fluidly between

Fuck me until I no longer know my
name
Until you against me is the only
rhythm beating within my veins
focus, focus now
You are all I see
Come on, give it to me
I'll make you see the stars if you
make me your star
You can try to hide, but the
memories will follow you wherever
you are

My quality of life is confined to a
sick mind
One that I can never replace or
change
Only feeding it a new med until it
finally goes to bed
I am possessed, I am plagued
All hopes of happiness waived

He left
Just like that, in a blink of an
eye, as simple as those two words
All the years and time washed down
the drain
My scent, my lips erased as my eyes
puddle like rain
All the love I have discarded in the
nearest bin
Waiting for recycle as he recreates
what we had in another woman that
sucked him in
he left
My soul ripped from my body
sobbing uncontrollably, begging for
him to stay
begging him to not throw me away
He did not bat an eye, he did not
tremble when he said there will
never be another you and I
he left
Just like that, quick as a soft
breeze
like the one that would touch my
skin lightly as I laid my head on
his chest in the summer heat

I search to stand back up but can
not find my feet
I have been beaten down, bruised
from defeat
he left
He couldn't deal with my
insecurities any longer
He gave up on everything we could be
The only man that I felt like ever
believed in me
I wore him down with my doubt, I
pushed him away too far this time
I would do anything to keep him for
a lifetime
but he left
And I cannot bear the feeling
I lay on my back and stare at the
ceiling
Clutching onto the covers where he
once laid
Praying that in his mind my memory
does not fade
he left

The clouds are whisked into cotton
candy swirls
I want to lay on them with you

I feel trapped by "I love you"
What do you actually want from me?

You don't have to respond, I can
feel the cold
I know that in your arms, I'm not
the one you hold
You search for something new off the
lot
I was the classic sitting in the
garage you forgot
I can't move the way you do,
I'll find peace in my loneliness, I
hope I see it through
I hope one day we cross paths again
Maybe both millionaires and I'll
take you for a spin
By then I'll be restored with a
fresh coat of paint
Full of love that isn't faint
I hate to see your life from a
distance
But I guess sometimes people take
the path of least resistance
And if you end up with a new life
and a baby
I'll try my best to not lose it and
go crazy
I'll do everything I can to be happy
for you
Because all I wanted was for your
dreams to come true

I know your head is a mess
I know you have things you'll never
confess
Let me make you feel free,
no costs no fees
You don't have to act strong when
you're in my arms
It's okay baby, silence your alarms
Come over, come stay the night
I promise I'll make you feel
alright
Let down your guard and open your
mind
And leave all of your worries behind

The way you feel inside of me sends
me over the moon
I feel you crash into my planet
sending a shockwave across my solar
system
You make me see stars in my eyes

I feel your heartbeat gently
Each beat reminds me I'm safe
And tucked away in your arms
I'm protected

This might be the last letter you
ever get from me
Maybe you'll see everything we could
be
Or maybe you'll let it go free
I've been talking to my preacher and
he said it isn't a myth
God doesn't give the weak hard
things to deal with, there's a
battle for everyone that we choose
to break bread with
Did you know in old Japanese culture
they'd fix broken glass with gold
seams?
Did you know that I supported every
last bit of your dreams?
See it's funny right, it's easier to
toss away something shattered
But in their eyes, they made it
still matter
Cause what's the point of something
manufactured, when you can see the
art in something once fractured
It tells a story,
Even though it was once broken now
it shines with glory
Something to tell your kids too,
And I'm ready to have one for you
I want to give your Mama grandkids
Your Granny great-grandkids

They would be so great, full of
brains and brilliance
See in everything hurting there's
still resilience
There's no shame in someone knowing
all of you
Even when the devil got you, I still
saw it through
We could go to the golden gate for
your birthday,
Spend a grand and call it payday
I saw the light in the darkness and
it painted a picture
I took my space and read the
scripture
I saw it in a dream, what it all
could be
But even then you said no more you
and me
I couldn't grasp the thought not
even for a second
My spot next to you got threatened
I no longer cared if you tried to
fuck me away,
Cause their love is nothing like the
kind I offer if you were to stay
You tell me not to cry
But you sucker punched me saying
goodbye

I'd pack your lunch every morning
You wrecked my world like a tornado
with no warning
In the pieces all I saw was you,
And I knew that it had to be love,
it must be true
Without hesitation, you're the only
one that's helped me find relaxation
I believed in you, full throttle
If you believe in me I'd be your
supermodel
I'm not going to beg, not a second
more
We were hot and heavy, now it's a
Cold War
I shed blood and tears for this battle
But if it's true love I'll ride it
out like in the saddle
so this is my last letter to you
hoping to win
I hope you never forget everything
that we could've been
And if you wave your white flag,
I hope you remember everything we had
I know I was insecure and scared
But my love and loyalty to you can
never be compared
Find peace in my pieces
I was for own, never on leases
You can't rent the realness I had
I'll always love you, good or bad

please never forget how much I
adored and loved you, or how I
would've done anything to have you
I hope she makes you feel special
and tastes sweeter than chocolate
fondue
The same sweet taste that you left
on my lips
The same soft feeling of your skin
on my fingertips
The same gentle moans that would
escape from me as you would rock
into my hips
I lost it all at the table and you
took off with my poker chips

What's left when you gave everything
and it wasn't enough

I don't know why I do this to myself

I don't know why I try to bury
myself

How sad is it to count your breaths
to know you've finally gone to sleep
so I can be free?

His heartbeat thudded slowly in his
sleep
I watched his chest rise and fall
with each peaceful breath
His lips looked soft and plush, I
wanted to kiss them but was too
afraid I might wake his dreamy
slumber
I wish I could count each perfect
eyelash and kiss his eyelids, for
behind them is the most mesmerizing
ocean deep eyes I have ever looked
into
Each beat of his heart was like sand
slipping out of an hourglass
Each grain was another second
slipping away from my grasp and
neared his leaving
Each breath a tick on a clock, an
unsettling reminder of how short our
time together would be once he woke
I pictured myself sitting at the
base of an hourglass with sand
seeping around me and through my
fingers as I tried to stop the flow
of time from suffocating my dreams
of laying by your side for just a
moment more
I watched you take a deep breath and
let tears well in my eyes, I do not
like goodbyes
How do you leave the man you adore?

Because I would rather fall asleep
in the arms of someone who does not
love me
Because it would make sense then to
feel so empty
Because falling asleep in the arms
of someone who loves me would be a
great injustice
Because every tender touch would be
a reminder
That I cannot love them fully
That I feel empty in between each
soft kiss
That I am numb
And they are noise to silence the
pain that bellows within me

Love your own soul the ways you
loved a man with no soul

You smile so deliciously for someone
who tore my heart out viciously

Ma
I'm tired
I know you won't hear or see this
But I'm tired
I'm tired of this life
The relentless repeat
The ridiculous ridicule
Ma
I'm tired
Not the tired that requires rest
The tired that requires peace
Why didn't you teach me what peace
was? Where can I find it?
Ma
I'm tired
Did you see my missed calls?
I was hanging by a thread, wasn't I
cut from your cloth?
I tried to sew myself together but
stuck my fingers instead
Ma
I'm tired
I want to go home but I don't know
what home is
Why didn't you teach me what home
was? Who it belongs to and what it
consists of? I know what it lacks
Ma
I'm tired
I don't know who the woman in the
mirror staring at me is
She takes up a lot of space and she
reminds me of you

Ma
I'm tired
You weren't ready for me
I see the child that was inside of
you still screaming to be free
Ma
I'm tired
Is the monster under my bed the same
one that's in your closet? I can
feel myself losing warmth and wonder
if that's what made you so cold
Ma
I'm tired
Do you see yourself in me? Is that
what makes you so sad? Is that why
I'm so sad?
Ma
I'm tired
You taught me how to be hungry
without letting my belly growl, but
I don't know how to feed myself
anything good
You see, you taught me how to be
independent, to not need anyone
except myself
But I don't know what to do with
this loneliness that hides behind
the bright lights of "I made it on
my own"
Ma
I'm tired

Why do you beat yourself black and
blue over "not feeling good enough"?
Let him GO

When I close my eyes to go to sleep
the faces of the women you betrayed
me for play like a projector in my
mind

My soul is broken
A clock trying to find the beat
It misses the count and then the
counterclockwise repeats
I think that I'm okay
That everything is fine
But every tick of time is a
countdown of detonation until I
completely unwind
I try to hold on
To grasp onto anything
But I am a falling angel
I've been clipped of my wings
I hit the pavement so hard it shakes
my body and comes out as sobs
I played my luck and lost against
the odds
I can't see anyone I love in my
reflection
I lost everything searching for
affection

I am so very sad inside
A black pit of turmoil
Please don't slip

I see you now only in my dreams
With the stroke of an artists brush,
I paint a hyper-realistic version of
   you that I can touch once more
I caress your cheek and run my thumb
across the scar near your soft nose
In the dream world I can see the you
         I thought you were
            it haunts me
I loved the man I thought you were,
but he's a shadow to who you became
And with that, the wind picks up and
   you fade into dust as the breeze
   hints at your laughter once more
I wonder how you can sleep without
         me in your arms now

Be careful who you waste time with
You might be making memories that
last a lifetime
While for them it'll be a faint blur

My screams begging for you to come
back
Wishing I could have jumped in the
way the second your car veered off
track
Broken and bloodied knuckles I wear
Each punch an angry plea
Angry that you've been taken away
from me
I scream and sob as I beat the
ground
How could anyone steal your crown?

I dream of you, my sunshine
I weep, for you left me behind
The clouds are grey and I feel lost
once again, but not the type that I
can find
It's within

I'm usually more of a Sunflower girl,
but Poinsettias will do in this cold

As I play the record I thrifted for
seventy-five cents over once more
I envision someone dancing in
their kitchen, copywritten
nineteen sixty-four
The bells chime, and the piano
crescendos as children giggle and
play
It's the Eve before the big
Christmas Day
nestled in my warm blanket a smile
spreads across my face
smiling at the thought of the holiday
meanings and all of their grace
Because seventy-five cents was all I
needed to feel thankful and blessed
I know this year has been unruly,
and nothing like the rest
But the music plays on, just like I
will for the many years to come
I know that it's okay that this year
might not have been the "one"
With each passing day, I've grown
more and more
I know that I'm more prepared for
the coming year than I ever have
been before
But for now, I'll settle with my hot
cocoa and glimmering lights
And hum along to the record playing
Silent Night

The warmth of your body was
inviting, your bottom lip I was
biting
The feeling of you on top of me,
your touch simple and carefree
My hands in your hair and down your
back, you sent my body off track
Our bodies collided
An occurrence that has left me
misguided
We laid in the sheets, worn out like
athletes
Champions of one another, a memory
hard to smother

Dip your hands into forbidden waters
Rock me back and forth like a ship
lost in your seas
Submerse me, drown me in your touch
You give me visions of waves
crashing as our bodies collide
You're as soft as a breeze
You're as rough as gale-force winds
You slam my shores, causing havoc,
forcing me to succumb to the immense
power that you hold over me
You launder me, calming me with your
gentle waters, you caress my fragile
body
You're my forbidden waters
I beg to touch, I breathe to see, I
cry to hold
Submerse me

Sometimes I feel like a heap of
nachos
Hot, cheesy, tasty, everyone pulls
me in every direction, taking what
they want, their hunger thieving
hands ripping me apart

I feel like I am scribbles
Messy patterns
Random twists and turns
Made out of frustration
Dancing with an uneasy anxious hurry
Other times they are made out of
soft swirls and lackadaisical
thoughts

Every hour with you is golden hour

I want to feel the sticky summer air
wrapped around us as I lay my head
on your shoulder
I want this now, no more waiting
until we're older
My curls a mess in the dripping
humidity, the smell of sweat and
jasmine in the breeze
I want to feel your love course
through me and bring me to my knees
Your hands on my thighs
You hold my chin and look me in my
eyes
My lips ache to kiss yours
I want my waves to crash against
your shores
I'm scared you'll run, but I'm done
hiding
I broke down my walls I'm done
fighting
So here I stand with the bits and
pieces I still recognize as me
Take me as you wish or just leave me
be
I don't want to wait or waste
I'm tired of feeling so displaced
I want to come home to see the
sunlight streaming in on your face
as you dance down the hall
I want to catch you no matter how
many times you fall
Tumble into my arms and I'll rock
you steady
Just tell me if you're ready

Watching you is like sitting by the
beach
The tide is your movement, rising
and falling
Falling and rising
Your shores keep me steady

I can't see anything I love in my
reflection
I lost myself searching for affection
I thought it was so special, the
perfect connection
In his arms I found protection
In my eyes, he was the definition of
perfection
But behind it all, I was just part
of a collection
At the time I was just a selection
I was never his only sweet
confection
And now I'm left in a state of
abjection
After the truth came out in a gut-
wrenching confession
I was sick for his love, plagued
with its infection
Making excuses for every mistake he
made as if I was responsible for
their correction
I look in the mirror and beg for a
resurrection
But I can't find a single thing I
like in my complexion

Stashed away
Hidden to stay
Memories rot
Trying to not give them any thought
Burrowed and hidden
Thinking about them is forbidden
They feed your emotions
And leave you drawing at the hands
of their oceans
Always filled full
You can feel those memories pull
Trying to get you to hear them
calling
Wanting you to come back crawling
They whisper your name
Wanting you to remember the sad
shame
They slowly fade
But not quick enough
Reminding you of those things that
hurt the most
They haunt you forever
Never letting you quite go
Even though it's the one thing you
wish you could sever

Wisped away in the breeze
Just another young girl on her knees
She would never speak of those days,
folded and tucked away deep into a
cage
Twelve birthday candles lit in a row
She watches them as they grow
The other children laugh and play
The last bit of sparkle in her eyes
disappears like the sunset on a bay

In my mind, you're always going to
leave
You'll always think of the best lies
for me to believe
With due time you'll go back to your
old ways
Your promise of honesty and loyalty
will be a phase
I gave you every part of me
I could've sworn we were meant to be
But who I thought you were was a
mask
And you could never tell the truth
no matter how many times I would ask
You went behind my back enough times
to break it
I tried to stand tall but I couldn't
take it
The man I saw you as is a stranger
to who you really are
You always had to take it too far
You were so desperate to fuck
everyone but me
You were so desperate to show them
everything I wanted to see

Some days I just lay in bed
The thoughts of you constantly
running through my head
Baby, I'm dying thinking of the
things I should have said
Like the first time you cut me
I should have said we were through
And maybe then I wouldn't be feeling
so blue

Crawling into a sea of covers you capsized me, letting me sink into a deep whirl of senses and emotions. You washed over me, covering me with your scent, your touch, your taste. It was refreshing, like petrichor; the smell of rain falling onto the dry Earth. It felt cleansing in a way, to have something new, to feel new. It was almost like the calm before the storm, I could *feel* the atmosphere changing, electrical charges pulsed in the air and through my body. My skin raised into goosebumps as if the temperature had suddenly dropped and a slight wind clutched my body.

You were the storm, sending fear into my veins, overturning me as if I were a stranded boat lost in the ocean. But once I began to sink into the waters that were you I was calm, delighted, reinvigorated. You laundered me softly, soft like morning dew gently rolling off of a rose petal. And suddenly I was at the bottom of the ocean looking up at you, smiling. It was an unexplainable phenomenon, I felt as if I could breathe underwater as long as I was in your presence. The feeling of having you surround me with your embrace and to feel your touch was staggering. I was drowning in you, but that was perfectly fine with me.

In hues of blues, I feel safe
and warm, surrounded by a fog of
serenity that tickles my nose and
kisses my toes
when I close my eyes I see visions
of you dancing away my fears and
holding me close

I feel as though there is a small
child stuck within me
Screaming and throwing a tantrum to
get out
I feel the mad man within me bang on
his cage
Shrieking to get out, grabbing at
the bars of my ribcage in an attempt
to break free
I feel them breaking me

I want the type of love that looks
at all of my shattered pieces and
does not view me as broken, but only
a beautiful puzzle waiting to be put
together
I want the type of love that sees
all of my chaotic colors splashed
across a canvas and does not view me
as a mess, but only a masterpiece
waiting to win first place at an art
gallery
I want the type of love that sees my
eyes become rivers of sadness and
does not evacuate but sees it as an
opportunity to rescue
I want the type of love that hears
my tornado of hate ravish my mind
and does not seek shelter but plays
over the warning sirens that I don't
want this type of love
I deserve it

Things I can't handle:
The scene photographs
The blood down the side of the car
Where I know you once hung out of
laughing
Your seat pushed back nearly to the
one behind it
I can't handle knowing that when
they got to you
You were cold
The warmth of your soul stolen in
the cold of the night
I can't handle the way it dripped
and smeared
The crunched metal
Your exploded chest
My exploded heart
I wish I could have told you how
much I loved you
And held your hand as we slipped
away together instead

I wish I could have wrapped you in
cloth
Pure white linen against your face
I wish I could have stroked your
cheeks and kissed your nose
I would have held you in my lap,
stroked your soft hair
Instead of wishing I knew the exact
date
To when I held you last

You're going away
And there's nothing I can say
To keep you from your departure
You have my heart strung across your
bow like an archer
We're growing apart
I can feel it deep inside my heart
I don't want you to go
But staying isn't the title of your
show
You're ready to get started with
your new life
With a job, a house, and maybe a
wife
But I'm stuck here
Losing you was always my worst fear
I try to not think of you leaving
But it leaves my heart heavy and
grieving
Time continues to count down
And every second I fall deeper under
the waters in which I drown

Maybe I can force it down
Shove it in the nooks and crannies
Press it in between pages like a
flower
And forget

I couldn't erase you if I tried
An eraser to my skin cannot compare
to the burn I feel from missing you
I am hollow
An open wound pleading to be dressed

As eager as the first blooms nearing
spring
It peeks through the Earth searching
for the sun
Not caring if the last breath of
winter whispers its frost around its
delicate flowers

An empty home
Full of children that act wild,
outside is where they roam
For inside those walls, they must
stay hidden
And to speak of love is forbidden
An empty cabinet
Full of hungry bellies and
abandonment
Sad eyes pierce into me
While they look up at their sister
trying to be everything a mother
should be
But the beast is asleep
So silently we move and herd
together like sheep
Trying to not disturb the soul that
has spiraled out of control
Filling all of her voids with poison
to feel whole

From day one I wanted you
I would have held you and always
been true
But it never worked out
So I let my dreams drift away with
doubt
Time passed by
And my heart once full of love was
dry
But then you saw me
The way I saw you long before and
felt it was meant to be
But with time passed came
consequences
But love had already taken down our
defenses
We became inseparable
To love each other, we were capable
You filled my heart once dry
With the promise of you and I
But with all things, we faltered
Although our feelings remained
unaltered
We had to bid farewell
And that my love, hurt like hell

Sometimes the anger within my soul
rumbles like thunder and spills over
like rain
The survivors say it sounded as if
they'd been hit by a freight train

You were like a breath of fresh air
But just like a breath of fresh air
You left me almost as soon as I took
you in
How do you erase the memories of
what you thought would be the
greatest moments?

I see the face of the woman you
caressed in the bed we share
I can sense the betrayal in the air
How much does she really know? You
must wonder
I know it all but I'm sure there is
more if I dug under
I know you slid into their DMs days
after my graduation
I know you lied to me and said it
was my imagination
I know you told her you wanted her
to sit on your face
Right after I finished eating my
birthday cake at your place
I know you yelled at me for being
insecure
When you were treating her like a
Queen on a world tour
I know I read everything I wish
you'd tell me
I know I saw everything I wish I
could be
I know you bought us all something
for Christmas
When you were the only thing on my
wishlist
I think I found myself in ten
different inboxes before I found mine
I dropped the phone, my neck feels
as if it's wrapped in wire twine

No matter how near or far
No matter where you are
My eyes the deepest oceans and
highest skies
I'll be wherever you go, my arms
in the wind that wraps around your
perfect face,
I'll be in the stars that sparkle in
your eyes
I'll hold you close with my blanket
of clouds and wish that I was laying
with you warm and sound
No matter how long, how far
Your sail ships can rest at my shore

Lightning dances in the sky
I want to run outside and let its
energy go through my body
Rain specks the window panes
It looks like a mosaic pattern of my
tears
The thunder shakes the house with
its booming cries
I feel his pain
It's empty, hollow, and sad looking
within my house without you here

I want to lay in your arms once more. I want to feel your warm breath dance across my bare skin. I want to feel your chest move up and down as each beautiful breath you take moves within you. I want you to move within me once more, and maybe this time not leave me feeling so empty afterward. You cross my mind more than my own self crosses my mind. I wonder where you are, how you are, what you're feeling at the exact moments I'm feeling so lost. I wonder if you're as happy as you seem to be or if you're putting on a show. But I can't help but feel the burning thoughts that you are way better with me away from you drip down my spine. I wasn't fair to you and now I pay. I pay with every white tooth that makes your perfect smile shine, for it tears me apart as if they were a row of shark teeth eating my innards out. I pay with your perfectly sculpted body, it looks as if it was made of clay, so soft, so smooth, so strong, every inch of you flows into the next creating a masterpiece.

A masterpiece of gold while I am glass, shattered when I threw myself onto you. It was my fault. I pay with every word you speak, the warm sounds you make, the lush laugh you laugh, every noise you make is like a warm blanket wrapped around me, but I doused it in gasoline and dropped a match. I am scarred from the burns I inflicted upon myself forever. The scars cover my skin, your name written in them, a reminder of all the mistakes I made. I want to smash my head against a wall, watch my brain spill out, and then pick up each piece and try to see if there is an answer tangled within like a fortune cookie. I scream within, screaming at myself, why was I such a mangled mess when I had you? I let myself get kicked around like a puck on ice, not caring who I went to or where I was being sent next. I knocked you out of my park like a home run, but instead of winning it made me lose you indefinitely and forced me to keep running the bases wondering if you'll suddenly come back over the fence and look me in the face once more. But you won't.

I wouldn't look at myself in the mirror and see my eyes, the dark circles underneath them, and how empty they are. They told me once that eyes were the gateway to someone's soul, so why do mine look so hollow and lost? Oh, God, your eyes. Your eyes. I pay. Your eyes were an ocean, dripping in color and mesmerized me. Now I drown, gasping for breath as you turn away from me, letting me be pulled deeper into the cold, unforgiving waters. It's all my fault. But then it was over. I ruined it all. I wanted to be enough for everyone, but I was doing it in all the wrong ways. I have never known what or who I am. But for a split second with you, it was as if everything spinning around me stopped instantaneously. It's like my life is an endless hurricane. Everything I build gets destroyed in front of my eyes, I am splintered by my own attempts of success. I am thrown into the swirling gale-force winds and knocked senselessly.

I am thrown into the air by the howling laughter of life and then suddenly, it's as if I'm in the eye of the storm. I plummet at a sickening rate, my stomach in my throat because the wet pavement is approaching too quickly. And then I hit. I hit so hard it rattles my bones, it rocks me down to my soul, it shatters my body. I force my swollen eyes open and look at the devastation, I frantically reach for the shards of my life, but they cut me. Everything I reach for cuts me, my hands are now gashed and bleeding, but I still reach to build something out of the shambles. I scream and sob as my body begs for me to stop, to give up, to just close my eyes forever. Just as I manage to piece together a part of me from the rubble the storm kicks back up and I am sent into the vigorous cycle of torture. Sometimes I close my eyes and just clench when it hurts the most. Sometimes I scream and beg for it to stop, trying to fight it. But no matter what I do, I hurt.

Erratic kitty
Jumping all around
Little bean paws
Cushion her when she jumps to the
ground
She plays and plays
Then sleeps away the rest of her
days
A soft queen
Running around in her ring
A circus act entertaining her guests
Finding things to play with along
her quest
Spotted and speckled, colorfully
striped
Her wild eyes, and her mama's hype

Sometimes my anxiety feels like a
bird trapped inside of a cage
There is something within me that
begs to escape
I try to act right but within my
shell of a body
I feel like a child lost within a
supermarket
Searching for help and only finding
strangers

I love you
I hope you know how often my mind
drifts to you and how often it makes
me smile
Waking up next to you has been one
of the most wonderful things
I love feeling the warmth of your
skin against mine
You're what makes a house feel like
home

I hope you never forget the love I
had for you
It was pure, full, and unconditional

Its slowly feeling you slip away
Feeling the annoyance
Feeling the exhaustion
Feeling you push me away
Feeling you wish that you could cut
me off but feeling like it may be too
hard
So you slowly shove me away
As I reach so desperately for you

I want the type of love full of
surprises
Little notes left for me to find
Kisses on my shoulder as you hold me
from behind
I want the type of love full of "I
saw this and thought of you"
A love never allowing me to second
guess my worth or where I stand
I want the type of love that will
keep me from harm's way with the
guide of their hand

When I first kissed you it was like anticipating the drop of a roller coaster, you know that it is coming, every inch of your body is tingling and ringing with excitement and nervousness all at the same time. Your lips were plush, warm, and inviting against mine. You took my breath away while breathing life into me. I was alive, I was at peace, yet my mind was racing. It was like you were a fountain full of liquid gold, you began to pour into me filling all of my missing pieces and cracks. I was glowing from the inside out, shimmering and radiating with your presence. I had always felt broken in a sense, not quite to one person's fault. I am most definitely always insecure and anxious about something.

But with you, for even a split second of you making me feel alive felt like someone ripping hundreds of pages out of my book of life and burning all of the wrong parts and writing happiness in like you would write "void" on a check. With you around, I did not allow my mind to think about all of the things I had convinced myself were wrong with me. I only thought of how your mouth moved to form the words, "You're gorgeous," or how your eyes would look into mine. Your eyes were deep oceans and your body was a riptide that pulled me away from the shore I thought was my safe haven, but in reality, was just my own false idea of security. I fell in love with the sea once you pulled me away, I was falling in love with you.

I see you in my sleep
Because that's the only place left
to love you

It's oddly warm for a mid-December
night
With a slight drizzle and a soft
breeze
I sat with my thoughts and sorted
them out one by one until I felt
right

Today I smiled
No really, I know it sounds awfully
silly
But I smiled

You know, the one where you show all
of your teeth without a care in the
world about what you look like in
your reflection?

The kind that sees the woman deep
inside you and denies any self-
rejection?

She loves you, and the way your eyes
light up when such happiness spreads
across your face
She knows your worth and makes you
remember you have a place
no matter if it's just a place for a
time or a moment
you belong right where you are and
you're going to own it

How could I begin to trust that you
won't hurt me
When I can't trust my own self to
not hurt me

I love you
I wish I could hold you and swim in
your soul
I wish we could have grown old
You were so pure
I love you

My mother taught me to not trust
women
Half the time I do not trust myself

You deserve the softest type of love. The kind that cannot be compared to plush pillows that your sleepy head rests against. So soft and gentle that it could make a cushion of clouds look hard. You deserve the strongest type of love. So strong that the toughest steel could not make a dent, strong enough to move mountains to make a path easiest for you to travel on. Strong enough to hold you high above ravishing waters, out of any harm's way, even if that means drowning to keep you safe. You deserve the type of love you never have to ask for. The type that holds you when you are too lost for words, the type that makes you your favorite meal without you ever saying you're hungry, the type that rubs your aching back without you ever saying it hurts. You deserve the type of love that never tries to change you, but is only your biggest supporter, cheering at the finish line because they know you can and will succeed. You are the greatest award anyone could receive. You deserve the type of love that never lets you doubt where you stand or your importance. You deserve the type of love that sees your kaleidoscope of colors and is completely enthralled, hanging onto every word you speak like it's the last bit of water dripping out of a dry faucet. You deserve a love fuller than the ocean. You deserve a love purer than the melting ice from a glacier. Your heart and soul are the purest white of snow falling from the skies, everyone around you squeals with excitement as you sprinkle your joy across their faces and they erupt in laughter. You deserve the type of love that fills you full of warmth on the coldest days, the type of love that is a refreshing glass of water on the hottest days. You deserve the type of love that tells you "I love you" in every little way and action without needing to actually say "I love you". You deserve the type of love that is malleable, full of elasticity, always able to fit the situation but able to snap back to the way it was before. You deserve a love full of growth, especially now. You are always going to be growing, becoming a person with more knowledge and experience, you deserve someone who can grow with you, not apart from you. You deserve a love that is unconditional. The type that knows all of your past, one that can take on every sharp corner and smooth curve and never judge, only accept. You deserve a love full of acceptance. You deserve a love that is unconditional. You deserve a love that has no terms and conditions that you must agree to, never a love full of commands and demands. You deserve a love that loves the 5 am you, hair matted down on one side and sticking straight up on the other from your slumber, you deserve a love that loves you at noon when you're eating like a starved wolf, and grinning with spices stuck in your teeth. You deserve a love that loves the 3 pm you, growing angsty and wanting off work, you deserve a love that loves the 7 pm you, hair wet and wild from a shower, you deserve a love that loves the 10 pm you, weary-eyed and trying to stay awake. You deserve a love that loves the Monday morning you just as much as the Friday night you. You deserve the type of love full of happiness and full of motivation. You deserve the love that loves all of you, at any given moment, unconditionally, endlessly, and without hesitation. Do not ever settle until you find this type of love, you are worthy

Some men are evil
I know
I have felt their hands grasp my
neck
They have taken things from me that
I'll never get back

But some men are loving
I know
I have felt their hands hold my
heart delicately
They have given me things that I
never imagined possible

I want to feel every inch of you
I want to feel you deep within my
soul

I wish we could ride in a spaceship
and go to the stars so I could watch
the galaxies sparkle in your eyes

I feel like I'm losing my mind while
everyone is trying to take a piece
of my mind

I need peace of mind

I don't owe you a thing
You brought me into this world
without my consent
I'm not responsible for fixing your
mistakes
A child is not born to fix what's
already broken
I'm not responsible for you caring
Or you getting to know me
Or you trying to be there
Actions
Will
Always
Prove
Louder
Than
The drunk 9 pm text of I love you
Means nothing to me
You can't even face your own
daughters
And fix us

You make me feel like a dainty baby
bumble bee who's just landed on her
first flower
You feel so soft and warm
I could lay here with you forever

The cool water danced between my
fingertips
The sound of the hushed rush puts my
thoughts at ease
I close my eyes
It feels as if I've stuck my hands
into a pile of silk ribbons
I cup the water in my hands and
brush it against my face
The water felt refreshing
Like a fresh start
Flowers of reds and purples played
hide and go seek along the bank of
the stream
They tangled themselves in morning
glory and other viney greens, their
blooms waved hello to the soft
breeze
I close my eyes
The sound of the hushed rush puts my
thoughts at ease

I used to cry when you'd leave,
Before I could pull myself out of
the crib that seemed more like a
cage,
You'd say you'd be right back,
you're going to the store, whatever
trick you had up your sleeve
I'd call out to you, wanting to be
held and comforted but I began to
realize you didn't like coming back
as I began to age
The memory of your car pulling
away, the sound of gravel, the rain
speckled windowpane, the cough of
exhaust as I watched you leave me
over and over
I stopped crying and asking why
I made friends with the monsters
under the bed, at least they would
play with me
I have wondered what you were up to
since age three

Somewhere between the lines of the
gas stations and friends with names
I'd never heard
I'd wait for dad to come home, maybe
he'd love me more than you preferred
I used to cry to make you come home
After my tears had dried and I
watched her leave knowing she had
lied
I'd play games and make bets, if the
bluebird flies away before I count to
ten I'll have my daddy home again!
But it never worked on red birds
for mommy, so I would sit for hours
watching the clock spin
Each tick was a piece of my heart
flaking away, the color slowly seeping
out of my soul and turning grey
Grey in my eyes, grey in my
reflection, a jumbled mess of
careless adults indiscretion

I feel so hollow inside
like I've been gutted out by life
and left to bleed out onto society

I never got to say all the ways you
made me feel

Your eyes remind me of the Earth
The dark rich soil that nurtures the
most beautiful flowers
Specks of gold flicker when caught
in the sunlight and dance like hot
embers
They remind me of the laughter from
a melting chocolate cone as it drips
down your smooth skin, you're the
center of a freshly baked brownie
that I ache to taste

To truly feel safe:
When I close my eyes
And the darkness slips over my hues
of blues
I do not tremble with fear that you
will stuff my mouth and tell me not
to scream
When I close my eyes
And the darkness slips over my
hues of blues I do not anticipate
crawling hands of disadvantage
stealing my soul in my slumber
When I close my eyes
And the darkness slips over my hues
of blues
I do not cover my head scared to
be beaten awake and sob under the
pillow
When I close my eyes
I feel safe
I feel warm
I feel surrounded by a fog of
serenity that tickles my nose and
kisses my toes
When I close my eyes and the
darkness slips over my hues of blues
I see visions of you dancing away my
fears and holding me dear

Snow speckled your eyelashes as we
laughed like children as we played
in the snow
Your nose was red and your cheeks
were flushed
I wish I could live in these moments
forever

I'm a little girl stuck screaming
inside this woman who seems foreign
to me

I'm free

Can't you see?
That huge smile that spreads across
my face
I finally found my place
I'm not who I was
Or who you thought I would be
I'm simply, and complexly me
You can't keep me bound to a town
that tried to make me drown
You kept me suffocated for years
under your thumb
Always worried about what might be
the outcome
I clawed at the concrete until it
finally cracked
And there's no way that I'll ever go
back

Because I'm me
I'm not who you wanted me to be
Who you wished to fail so badly
Who you pushed around to the point
of wanting to end their life sadly
I'm not those things, those words
And to be honest, that shit was for
the birds
I can't believe I allowed myself to
be shrunk down to your size
You couldn't let me see that I could
win first prize
It intimidated you that I didn't care

And somewhere along the lines, to
you, that wasn't fair
So you chained me into a corner and
poked sticks
Your typical small-town circus act
to get a fix
I finally escaped your jaws, even
though you keep biting
And I know that it infuriates you to
watch me keep fighting
You can't make peace by taking away
every piece that creates a being
You can't live blindly and insist
that you're seeing
You failed me and many others
Because we refused to conform into
the towns next mothers
So you had to break us into pieces
so that you could try to swallow our
souls
You tried to convince us that our
ideas weren't real, that we had no
goals
But we are far much more than a
speck on the map
we realized your games and ran from
your trap

I'm free

Can't you see?

I know I'm not alone because you
painted a purple sunset for me on
the days I miss you most
You always know how to make someone
smile
You are the brightest star shining
in the night sky
You offered friendship to those who
thought they had no friends
You faced all of your trials and
tribulations with a smile even when
it hurt
I play your laugh over and over from
old videos, smiling till my eyes
blur
I miss you
Your energy, your smile
No one ever prepares you for the
quietness of losing a friend
The unanswered calls
The gut-wrenching voicemails
The hundreds of please don't be true
Please
Please, not you
But they never go through
And I wish I could have gone with
you
But now I stay here staring up at
the picture you painted for us to
all see
And I know that you're right here
with me

Sometimes when it's too hard to bear
I break out the beer
so I can taste once more what it was
like to have your lips around mine
on a hot summer night

I'll be wherever you go my arms in
the wind that wraps around your
perfect face

I hope I coated you in something
more than the coal you left on me

I met a man today, one I finally
liked
His name was Roy G Biv and he
showed me the rainbow
He told me not to worry, that I was
his child
He said it's okay to kiss women and
run wild
That I don't have to pick a side
unless I want too
He told me there are no sides to
love if it's true
That I can like any color, pink or
blue
Sometimes we're violet and yellow
But regardless I'll always say hello
We're children of the rainbow
The aftermath of the storm that
shines in the sky
The hell in the closet you tried to
shut out and question "why?"
Nothing is wrong with me, I love the
way each color has its own special
shine
When it comes to finding yourself, it
takes time

You wouldn't go
I asked you to come
So I went by myself
You called me furious so I said I
would come home
Now you're mad I'm coming home
I came home
Now you're mad I came home
I tried to reason with you
You told me it's all in my head and
I'm awful
I tried to give you space now you're
mad I'm not giving you the attention
you don't want, but do
You yelled at me and said you don't
care
I asked, about me?
You shouted of course and stormed
out of the room
Then came back and shook your finger
and reminded me that I was the
one who decided to go alone, so
therefore I must want to be alone
You left me crying all dressed up
Tears streaking the makeup I put on
to feel beautiful enough for you
To make you want me
But I just end up alone
I chase for the light at the end of
the tunnel
But every time you trick me with
your gaslight

You make me the happiest I've ever
been
You hold my head up high and kiss
me to remind me that I deserve this
love
I did not deserve my past
But you are set on making my future
bright
And I can never repay you for that
type of love
So thank you

Instead of wiping my tears like a
Queen deserves
You made me feel like a peasant,
pathetic for feeling

no one wants to talk about
How exhausting it is
To be unwell
In the midst of caring for others
who are also mentally unwell
Because it does not matter how awful
you feel
They feel worse
Their needs must be met
Or else you may lose them
And then it will be your fault
For not trying hard enough
For not being there
When all you have ever done is try
and be there
But you understand why they are
unwell
Because you are unwell
And you know what they're feeling
Because you feel it too

But you never speak of it because
they turn to you
For hope
For answers
In the midst of your own drowning,
you smile and reach for them
Even when it means being held under
the water to keep their head above
yours
You keep kicking to keep them up
Up, up, up
You can't give up
You have to keep kicking no matter
how exhausted your bruised body has
become
No matter how badly you just want to
breathe
You have to keep them up or they
will drown
But either way, I drown
Trying to keep them above the waters
that they wish to drown in

I love her
The sharp edges and curved corners
The way her belly rolls when she
sits and her thighs smush
I love her
She walks me through this life and I
must love her
May you never rely on someone to
love you
Before you learn to love yourself
Because the world will eat you up
and spit you out
It will fill your head with poisonous
thoughts of hatred towards yourself
You must fight the venom of society
You must love yourself

The person that could ruin my own
life is staring right back at me in
the mirror
A draw
Who shoots first?

The silent treatment
There are so many things you could
say
There are so many other things you
could do
You could sit down and explain to me
You could sit down and help me
understand
But instead, it's silence
With my mind racing
Wondering what I did wrong
Why it was wrong
How it was wrong
If anything is even wrong to begin
with
And trying to analyze the silence
into a solution
But you offer no help with your
coldness
You offer no help with your solitary
confinement
I don't want to be in your psych
ward any longer

I surrendered myself to keep you who
you are
A glass sucked dry
Shattering at your every word

I raised my voice because I didn't
feel heard

You raised your voice because you
didn't feel obeyed

If you do anything today, please
promise me
That you'll get up and look at
yourself in the mirror
And say "I love you"
You deserve to love yourself

I wore a pair of earrings that were
another woman's
Because you had convinced me I had
left them
Manipulation without hesitation
A monster in exchange for a man

A piece of glass with a display
separating us
Dividing Us
You hide behind your screen
Saying all of those things you
"don't mean"
You act like I don't see, then you
flash your fake grin at me
It's such a wild world we live in
Where we use words on screens to buy
power
And sit around the clock, refreshing
by the hour

Today I helped a mother move her
child out
My best friend
Their mother was crying and soaking
up every last second with her
precious baby
I wanted to cry
For how much she loves her child
And for how I left without goodbye
kisses
Or new towels and good omens
I did it myself
When I didn't have too
And I didn't realize until today
How important mothers are in every
little moment
And how I wish you would have been
their for mine

I forced myself to stop thinking
about what happened to me
And changed the narrative to what
could happen to me
How beautiful this life can be
How many possibilities there are
What was out of my control will
always be part of my story
But the rest I get to write myself

Oh, sweetheart,
Don't pay those cruel souls any
attention
The things they say about you are
projections of their own delusions
Threatened by your diamond mind

I forgive you
I forgive myself
For allowing you to hurt me
I will only rebuild from here
And I do not need your "helping
hand"

I will no longer allow myself to
feel such hatred for myself

It's about achieving your highest
point
Not worrying about theirs

Smile
Feel the Earth
You're alive, baby

You mean the moon to me
I know sometimes you go away
But you always come around again
with your phases

If you made it this far
Thank You
I hope you know that your story is
valid, I found freedom in speaking
my truths
Feelings are valid
Emotions are valid
You are valid

This world can be so cruel, yet so
beautiful. Keep your head high, take
time to feel the grass on your feet,
and smile in the sunshine

It gets better baby

Love Always

MIK

National Sexual Assault Hotline
1-800-656-HOPE (4673)

National Child Abuse Hotline
1-800-4-A-CHILD (422-4453)

National Domestic Violence Hotline
1-800-799-SAFE (7233)

Drug Abuse National Helpline
1-800-662-4357

GriefShare
1-800-395-5755

National Hopeline Network
1-800-SUICIDE
(784-2433)

National Suicide Prevention Hotline
800-273-8255

About the Author:

Morgan Irene Kinney is a jack of all trades. She works in construction but can fit and mold to any situation. She uses writing as her outlet for the journeys that life brings, and finds it very inspiring to hear that her words make others feel less alone. Her inspirations are all who have helped her go through things while she was going through them. She believes everyone should be there for one another as they experience life. She loves nature and being outside, anything artsy, and things she can create with her bare hands. She has two cats, Wall- E and Eva, and is a softy for any animal. She cares deeply.

CPSIA information can be obtained
at www.ICGtesting.com
Printed in the USA
LVHW081141011221
704823LV00008B/365

9 781638 378440